THE
BEACH
BOYS

MELODY LINE, CHORDS AND LYRICS
FOR KEYBOARD • GUITAR • VOCAL

HAL•LEONARD®

ISBN-13: 978-0-634-06284-1
ISBN-10: 0-634-06284-0

HAL•LEONARD®
CORPORATION
7777 W. BLUEMOUND RD. P.O. BOX 13819 MILWAUKEE, WI 53213

Visit Hal Leonard Online at
www.halleonard.com

Welcome to the PAPERBACK SONGS® SERIES.

Do you play piano, guitar, electronic keyboard, sing or play any instrument for that matter? If so, this handy "pocket tune" book is for you.

The concise, one-line music notation consists of:

MELODY, LYRICS & CHORD SYMBOLS

Whether strumming the chords on guitar, "faking" an arrangement on piano/keyboard or singing the lyrics, these fake book style arrangements can be enjoyed at any experience level – hobbyist to professional.

The musical skills necessary to successfully use this book are minimal. If you play guitar and need some help with chords, a basic chord chart is included at the back of the book.

While playing and singing is the first thing that comes to mind when using this book, it can also serve as a compact, comprehensive reference guide.

However you choose to use this PAPERBACK SONGS® SERIES book, by all means have fun!

CONTENTS

ALL SUMMER LONG

Words and Music by BRIAN WILSON
and MIKE LOVE

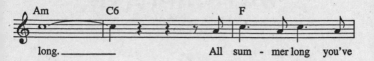

long. _____ All sum - mer long you've

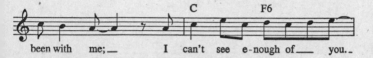

been with me; ___ I can't see e-nough of ___ you. _

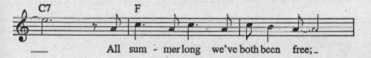

___ All sum - mer long we've both been free; _

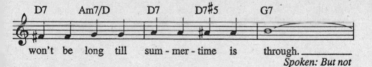

won't be long till sum - mer - time is through. _____

Spoken: But not

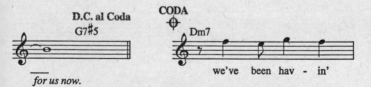

for us now. we've been hav - in'

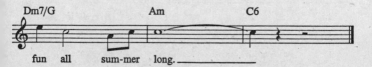

fun all sum-mer long. _____

BARBARA ANN

Words and Music by
FRED FASSERT

Bright Rock tempo

(Ba, ba, -ba, bar,___ Ba' - 'bra Ann.

Ba, ba, -ba, bar,___ Ba' - 'bra Ann.) Bar - bra

Ann,_____ take___ my

hand._____ Bar - bra

Ann,_____ you got me

rock-in' and a-roll-in', rock - in' and a-reel-in', Bar-bra

BE TRUE TO YOUR SCHOOL

Words and Music by BRIAN WILSON
and MIKE LOVE

Slowly

When some loud brag - gart tries to
let - ter - man's sweat - er with the
Fri - day we'll be jacked up on the

put me down__ and says his school is great,__
let - ters in front__ I get from foot-ball and track.__
foot-ball game__ and I'll be read - y to fight.__

I tell him right a - way now
I'm proud to wear it now when
We're gon - na smash 'em now, my

what's the mat - ter Bud - dy ain't you
I cruise a - round__ the oth - er
girl __ will be work - 'in on her

heard of my school? It's num-ber one in the state.__
parts of the town.__ I got my de - cal in back.__
pom-poms now,__ and she'll be yell-'in to - night.__

CABINESSENCE

Words and Music by BRIAN WILSON
and VAN DYKE PARKS

Light the lamp and __ fire __ mel-low
I want to watch you, __ wind-blown, fac-ing

cab-in es-sence; __ time-ly hel-lo
waves of wheat for __ your em-brac-ing.

wel-comes the time __ for a change.
Folks sing a song __ of the grange.

Lost and found, you
Nes-tled in a __

__ still re-main there.
__ kiss be-low there,

You'll find a mead-ow
the con-stel-la-tions __

__ filled with rain there.
__ ebb and flow there

I'll give you a
and wit-ness our

home ____ on the range. ____
home ____ on the range. ____

Faster (♩♩ = ♩♩)

Who ran the i - ron horse? Who ran the

i - ron horse? Who ran the i - ron horse?

Who ran the i - ron horse? Who ran the

i - ron horse? Who ran the i - ron horse?

Who ran the i - ron horse? Who ran the

i - ron horse? Who ran the i - ron horse?

Who ran the i - ron horse? ____

14

CALIFORNIA GIRLS

Words and Music by BRIAN WILSON
and MIKE LOVE

Moderate Shuffle Rock

CAROLINE, NO

**Words and Music by BRIAN WILSON
and TONY ASHER**

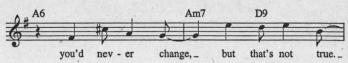

you'd nev - er change, _ but that's not true. _

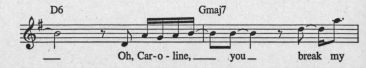

_ Oh, Car-o - line, _____ you _ break my

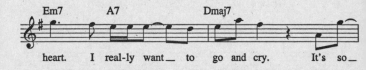

heart. I real-ly want _ to go and cry. It's so _

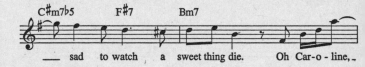

_ sad to watch a sweet thing die. Oh Car-o - line, _

_ why? _ Could I ev - er find in

you a - gain _____ things that made me love you

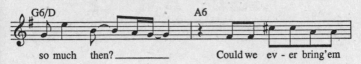

so much then?___ Could we ev - er bring 'em

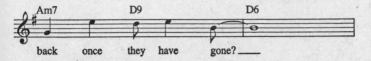

back once they have gone.___

Oh Car - o - line,___ no.___

(Instrumental)

Repeat and Fade

CATCH A WAVE

Words and Music by BRIAN WILSON
and MIKE LOVE

Moderately fast

Throw me a fa - vor, try the
Not____ just a fad____ 'cause it's
So____ take a les - son from a

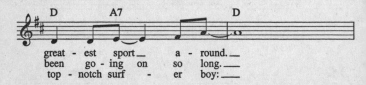

great - est sport___ a - round.___
been go - ing on so long.___
top - notch surf - er boy:___

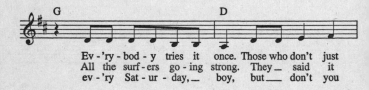

Ev - 'ry - bod - y tries it once. Those who don't just
All the surf - ers go - ing strong. They__ said it
ev - 'ry Sat - ur - day,__ boy, but__ don't you

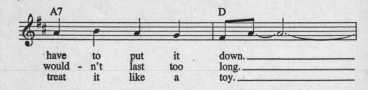

have to put it down._____
would - n't last too long._____
treat it like a toy._____

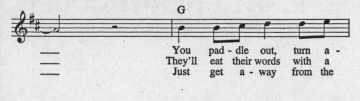

You pad - dle out, turn a -
They'll eat their words with a
Just get a - way from the

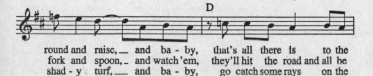

round and raise, __ and ba - by, that's all there is to the
fork and spoon, __ and watch 'em, they'll hit the road and all be
shad - y turf, __ and ba - by, go catch some rays on the

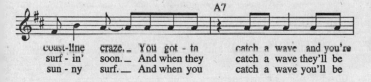

coast-line craze. __ You got - ta catch a wave and you're
surf - in' soon. __ And when they catch a wave they'll be
sun - ny surf. __ And when you catch a wave you'll be

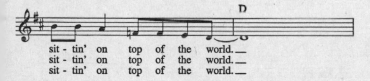

sit - tin' on top of the world. __
sit - tin' on top of the world. __
sit - tin' on top of the world. __

CHERRY CHERRY COUPE

**Words and Music by BRIAN WILSON
and ROGER CHRISTIAN**

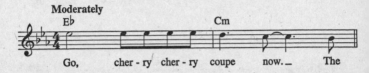

Moderately

E♭   Cm

Go,   cher - ry cher - ry coupe   now. _   The

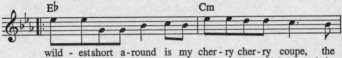

E♭   Cm

wild - est short a - round is my cher - ry cher - ry coupe, the
Chrome re - verse wheels and _ white - wall slicks, _ and it
coupe's _ tuck and roll un - der - neath _ the hood, and   the

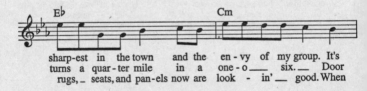

E♭   Cm

sharp - est in the town and the en - vy of my group. It's
turns a quar - ter mile in a one - o _ six. _ Door
rugs, _ seats, and pan - els now are look - in' _ good. When

A♭

one of its kind and it real - ly looks good, chopped
han - dles are off but you know I'll nev - er miss 'em. They
I go look - in' for some - thin' to do, it's

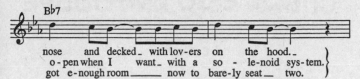

nose and decked with lov-ers on the hood.
o-pen when I want with a so-le-noid sys-tem.
got e-nough room now to bare-ly seat two.

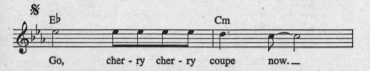

Go, cher-ry cher-ry coupe now.

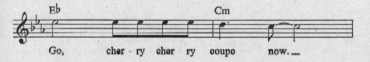

Go, cher-ry cher-ry coupe now.

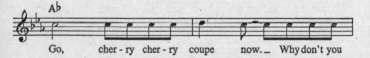

Go, cher-ry cher-ry coupe now. Why don't you

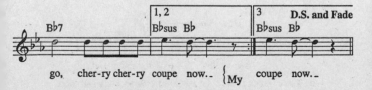

go, cher-ry cher-ry coupe now. My coupe now.

COME GO WITH ME

Words and Music by
C.E. QUICK

me. _____ Yes, I need you,

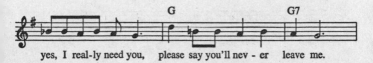

yes, I real-ly need you, please say you'll nev - er leave me.

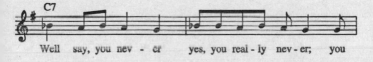

Well say, you nev - er yes, you real - ly nev - er; you

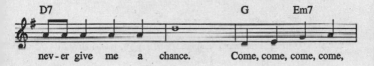

nev - er give me a chance. Come, come, come, come,

come in - to ___ my heart, _ tell me dar - lin',

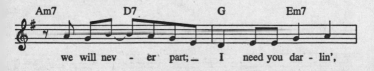

we will nev - er part; ___ I need you dar - lin',

so come go ___ with me. _____

COTTON FIELDS
(The Cotton Song)

Words and Music by
HUDDIE LEDBETTER

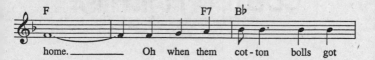

home. _____ Oh when them cot-ton bolls got

rot-ten you could-n't pick ver - y much cot-ton. In them

old cot-ton fields at home. _____

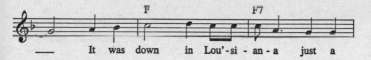

_____ It was down in Lou'-si-an-a just a

mile from Tex - ar - ka - na. And them old, old __

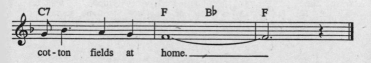

cot-ton fields at home. _____

CUSTOM MACHINE

Words and Music by BRIAN WILSON
and MIKE LOVE

Check my cus - tom ma - chine. _____

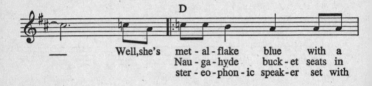

Well, she's met - al - flake blue with a
Nau - ga - hyde buck - et seats in
ster - e - o - phon - ic speak - er set with

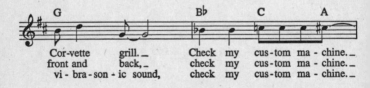

Cor - vette grill. _ Check my cus - tom ma - chine. _
front and back, _ check my cus - tom ma - chine. _
vi - bra - son - ic sound, check my cus - tom ma - chine. _

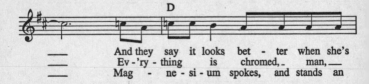

And they say it looks bet - ter when she's
Ev - 'ry - thing is chromed, _ man, _
Mag - ne - si - um spokes, and stands an

stand-in' still.
e-ven my jack.
inch off the ground.

Check my cus-tom ma - chine.

When I

step on the gus she goes wah.

I'll

let you look, but don't touch my cus-tom ma - chine.

Well, with

Repeat and Fade

(Instrumental)

DANCE, DANCE, DANCE

Words and Music by BRIAN WILSON,
CARL WILSON and MIKE LOVE

Moderate Rock

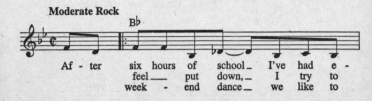

Af - ter   six hours   of   school __ I've had e-
feel __   put   down, __ I   try   to
week - end   dance __ we   like   to

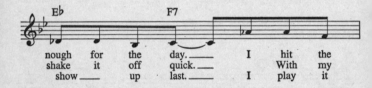

nough   for   the   day. __   I   hit   the
shake   it   off   quick. __   With   my
show __ up   last. __   I   play   it

ra - di - o   dial __   and   turn   it
chick   by   my   side, __   the   ra - di-
cool   when   it's   slow __   and   jump

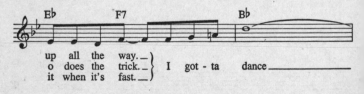

up   all   the   way. __ } I   got - ta   dance __
o   does   the   trick. __
it   when   it's   fast. __

DARLIN'

Words and Music by BRIAN WILSON
and MIKE LOVE

Moderately

Fm7   Eb   F7

(Instrumental)

> You know,   if
> I was liv-ing like

Cm7   F

words could say, —   that dar-ling I'd
half a man; —   then I could-n't love, but

Cm7   F7

find a way —   to let you know what you
now I can. —   You pick me up when I'm

Bb   F7

meant to me. _____   Guess it was
feel-ing sad, _____   more so than

Bb   G7

meant to be. _____   I hold you
I ev-er had. _____   Gon-na love you ev-'ry

DO IT AGAIN

Words and Music by BRIAN WILSON
and MIKE LOVE

With a solid beat

It's au-to-mat-ic when I talk with old friends and

con-ver-sa-tion turns to girls we knew, when their

hair was soft and long, and the beach was the

place to go. ___ The

sun-tanned bod-ies and waves of sun-shine, the
I've been think-ing 'bout all the plac-es we've

Cal - i - for - nia girls and a beau - ti - ful coast - line with
surfed and danced _ and all _____ the fac - es we've

Ab   Bb   To Coda

warmed - up weath - er; let's get to - geth - er and
missed. So let's get back to - geth - er and

Eb

do it a - gain. _

Ab   Cm7

With a girl the lone - ly sea looks good with

Fm7   Ab   Gm

moon - light; makes your night times warm and

Ab/Bb   Bb   D.S. al Coda

out of sight. _____ Well

CODA

Eb   Ab/Eb Eb

do it a - gain. _____

DO YOU REMEMBER?

Words and Music by BRIAN WILSON
and MIKE LOVE

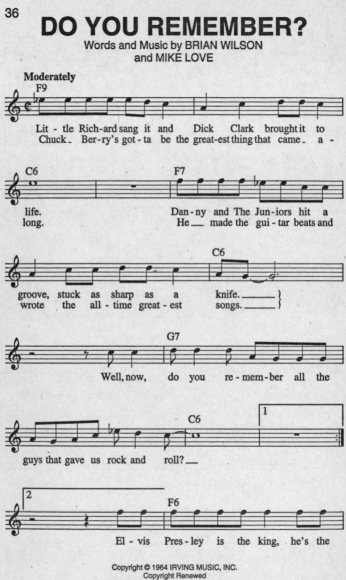

37

DO YOU WANT TO DANCE?

Words and Music by
BOBBY FREEMAN

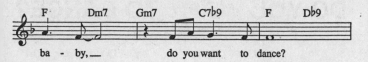
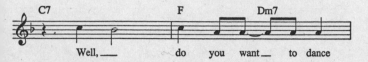
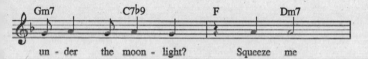

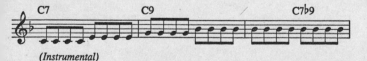
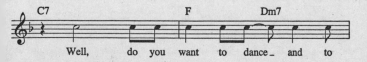

DON'T BACK DOWN

Words and Music by BRIAN WILSON
and MIKE LOVE

Moderately

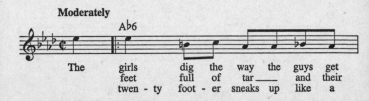

The   girls   dig the way the guys get
feet   full of   tar____ and their
twen - ty foot - er sneaks up like a

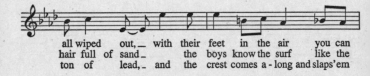

all wiped out, _ with their feet in the air you can
hair full of sand_   the boys know the surf   like the
ton of lead,_ and the crest comes a - long and slaps'em

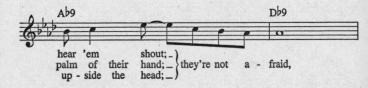

hear 'em   shout; _
palm of their hand; _ } they're not a - fraid,
up - side the head; _

not my boys. _____   They

grit their teeth, _____ they don't back

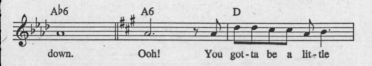

down. Ooh! You got-ta be a lit-tle

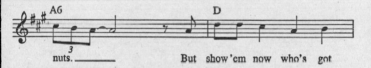

nuts. _____ But show 'em now who's got

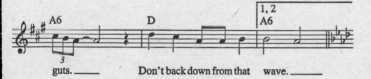

guts. _____ Don't back down from that wave. _____

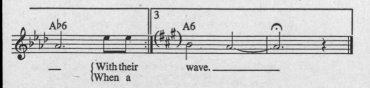

— { With their wave. _____
  { When a

DON'T WORRY BABY

Words and Music by BRIAN WILSON
and ROGER CHRISTIAN

Moderate Rock tempo

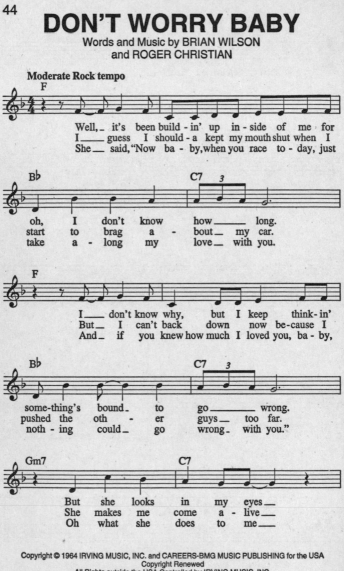

Well, — it's been build-in' up in-side of me for
I — guess I should-a kept my mouth shut when I
She — said, "Now ba - by, when you race to - day, just

oh, I don't know how long.
start to brag a - bout my car.
take a - long my love with you.

I — don't know why, but I keep think-in'
But — I can't back down now be-cause I
And — if you knew how much I loved you, ba - by,

some-thing's bound to go wrong.
pushed the oth - er guys too far.
noth - ing could go wrong with you."

But she looks in my eyes
She makes me come a - live
Oh what she does to me

DRIVE IN

Words and Music by BRIAN WILSON
and MIKE LOVE

Moderately

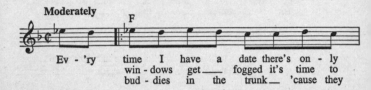

Ev - 'ry time I have a date there's on - ly
win - dows get___ fogged it's time to
bud - dies in the trunk___ 'cause they

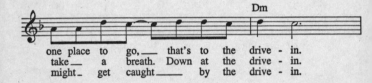

one place to go, ___ that's to the drive - in.
take___ a breath. Down at the drive - in.
might___ get caught___ by the drive - in.

It's such a pret - ty place to talk, and may - be
Or the cat___ dressed in white 'll scare you
And they'd look___ kind - a stu - pid get - tin'

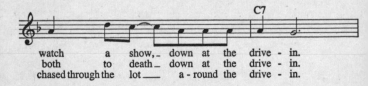

watch a show, ___ down at the drive - in.
both to death___ down at the drive - in.
chased through the lot ___ a - round the drive - in.

47

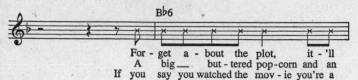

Bb6

For - get a - bout the plot, it - 'll
A big_ but - tered pop-corn and an
If you say you watched the mov - ie you're a

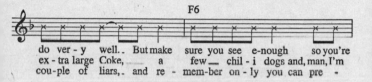

F6

do ver - y well._ But make sure you see e - nough so you're
ex - tra large Coke, a few_ chil - i dogs and, man, I'm
cou-ple of liars,_ and re - mem-ber on - ly you can pre -

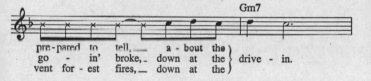

Gm7

pre - pared to tell,_ a - bout the ⎫
go - in' broke,_ down at the ⎬ drive - in.
vent for - est fires,_ down at the ⎭

C9   **F6**

I love the drive - in.

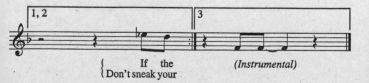

1, 2   **3**

If the   *(Instrumental)*
Don't sneak your

409

Words and Music by BRIAN WILSON,
GARY USHER and MIKE LOVE

be a time, —}
fast - est time. —}

(Gid - dy up, gid - dy up,

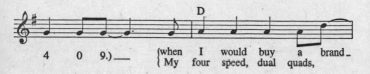

4 0 9.) —

{when I would buy a brand —
{My four speed, dual quads,

C   G
                    (4 0   9, —

— new 4 0 9.
Pos - i - trac - tion 4 0 9. _____

4 0 9, —   4 0 9, —

—}   Gid - dy up,   gid - dy up,

4 0 9, —   gid - dy up, gid - dy up,

gid - dy up,   4 0 9,

4 0 9, —   C
                  4 0 9, —

gid - dy up,   4 0 9,

50

gid - dy up, 4 0 9,

gid - dy up, 4 0... Noth - ing can catch her,

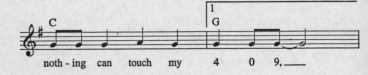

noth - ing can touch my 4 0 9, ___

4 0 9. ___ 4 0 9, ___ 4 0 9. ___

(4 0 9, ___ 4 0 9.) ___

Gid - dy up, 4 0

Repeat and Fade

(4 0 9, ___ 4 0 9.) ___

9. Gid - dy up, 4 0

FRIENDS

**Words and Music by BRIAN WILSON, CARL WILSON,
DENNIS WILSON and AL JARDINE**

52

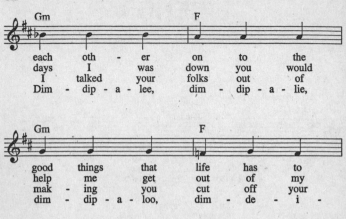

each   oth - er   on   to   the
days   I   was   down   you   would
I   talked   your   folks   out   of
Dim - dip - a - lee,   dim - dip - a - lie,

good   things   that   life   has   to
help   me   get   out   has   of   my
mak - ing   you   cut   off   your
dim - dip - a - loo,   dim - de - i -

give. }
hole. }
hair. }
o. }

(Instrumental)

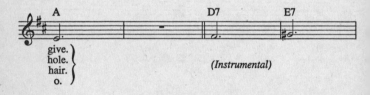

4th time To Coda ⊕ | **1, 3**

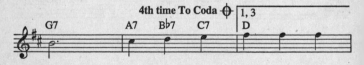

| **2**

Ah. _____

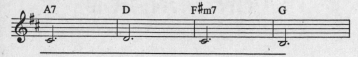

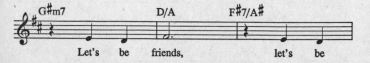

G#m7   D/A   F#7/A#

Let's be friends,   let's be

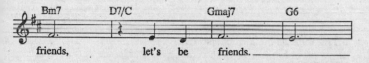

friends,   let's be friends. _____

D.C. al Coda
(take 3rd ending)   CODA

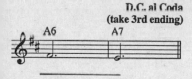

(Instrumental)

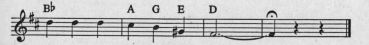

FUN, FUN, FUN

Words and Music by BRIAN WILSON
and MIKE LOVE

now. now. } And she'll have

fun, fun, fun, till her dad-dy takes the T-Bird a-way.

Well, the

A-well, you knew all a-long__ that your

dad was get-tin' wise to you__ now.__

And since he took your set of keys you've been

think-in' that your fun is all through__

now._____   But you can

come a - long with me, 'cause we got - ta lot - ta things to do__

_____ now._____   And   you'll   have

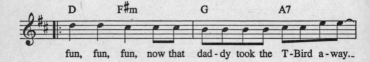

fun, fun, fun, now that dad - dy took the T - Bird a - way.__

_____   And   you'll   have

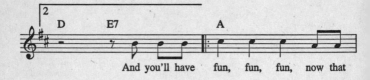

And you'll have   fun, fun, fun, now that

Repeat and Fade

dad - dy took the T - Bird a - way.__

GIRL DON'T TELL ME

Words and Music by
BRIAN WILSON

58

You did-n't an-swer my let-ter so I fig-ured it was__ just a lie._____

I'll see you this sum-mer and for-get you when I__ go back to Your school._____

Girl, don't tell me you'll write,__

Girl, don't tell me you'll write,__

Girl, don't tell me you'll write__

__ me a-gain__ this____ time.

GIRLS ON THE BEACH

Words and Music by BRIAN WILSON
and MIKE LOVE

Slow Rock beat

On the beach you'll find them there, in the sun and
How we love to lie a-round girls with tans of

salt-y air. The girls on the beach are
gold-en brown. The girls on the beach are

all with-in reach, if you know what to
all with-in reach, and one waits there for

do. you. Girls on the beach.

The sun in her hair, the

60

GOD ONLY KNOWS

Words and Music by BRIAN WILSON
and TONY ASHER

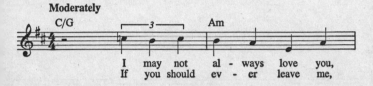

Moderately

C/G — 3 — Am

I may not al-ways love you,
If you should ev-er leave me,

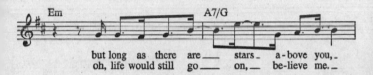

Em — A7/G

but long as there are___ stars___ a-bove you,___
oh, life would still go___ on,___ be-lieve me.___

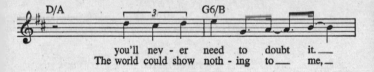

D/A — 3 — G6/B

you'll nev-er need to doubt it.___
The world could show noth-ing to___ me,___

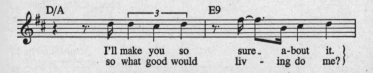

D/A — 3 — E9

I'll make you so sure a-bout it. }
so what good would liv-ing do me? }

G   D/F#

God on-ly knows_ what I'd be with-out_

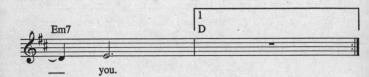

Em7   1. D

_ you.

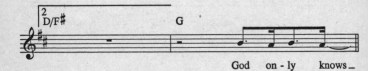

2. D/F#   G

God on-ly knows_

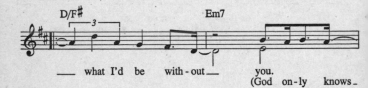

D/F#   Em7

_ what I'd be with-out_ you.
(God on-ly knows_

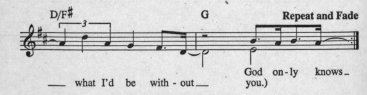

D/F#   G   **Repeat and Fade**

_ what I'd be with-out_ you.)
God on-ly knows_

GOOD VIBRATIONS

Words and Music by BRIAN WILSON
and MIKE LOVE

Light Rock

I, _____ I love the col - or - ful
Close my eyes. She's some - how

clothes she wears, _____ and _____ the
clos - er now. _____

way the sun - light plays up - on her hair.
Soft - ly smile. I know she must be kind. _____

I _____ hear the sound of a
Then _____ I look

gen - tle word, _____ on _____ the
in her eyes. _____ She _____ goes

wind that lifts her per - fume through the air. _____
with me to a blos - som world. _____

I'm pick - ing up good vi - bra - tions.

HAWAII

Words and Music by BRIAN WILSON
and MIKE LOVE

Moderately

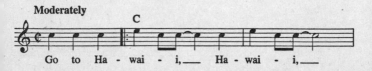

Go to Ha - wai - i, ___ Ha - wai - i, ___

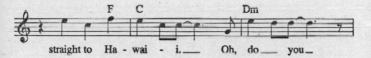

straight to Ha - wai - i. ___ Oh, do ___ you ___

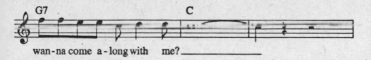

wan-na come a - long with me? _____

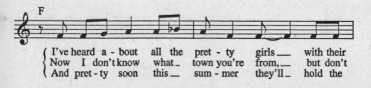

I've heard a - bout all the pret - ty girls ___ with their
Now I don't know what ___ town you're from, ___ but don't
And pret - ty soon this ___ sum - mer they'll ___ hold the

HELP ME RHONDA

Words and Music by BRIAN WILSON
and MIKE LOVE

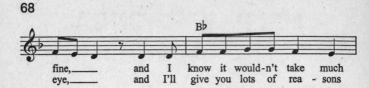

fine,_____ and I know it would-n't take much
eye,_____ and I'll give you lots of rea - sons

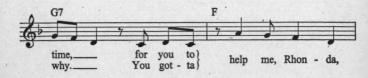

time,_____ for you to }
why._____ You got-ta } help me, Rhon - da,

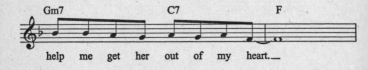

help me get her out of my heart.___

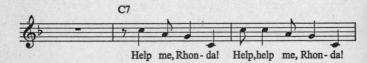

Help me, Rhon-da! Help, help me, Rhon-da!

Help me, Rhon - da! Help, help me, Rhon - da!

Help me, Rhon - da! Help, help me, Rhon - da!

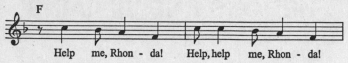

Help me, Rhon - da! Help, help me, Rhon - da!

Help me, Rhon - da! Help, help me, Rhon - da!

Help me, Rhon - da! Help, help me, Rhon - da!

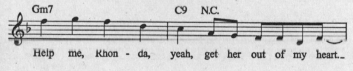

Help me, Rhon - da, yeah, get her out of my heart. __

She was __

Help me, Rhon - da! Help, help me, Rhon - da!

Help me, Rhon - da! Help, help me, Rhon - da!

HEROES AND VILLAINS

Words and Music by BRIAN WILSON
and VAN DYKE PARKS

Moderately fast

I been in this town___ so long that
Once___ at night___ Ca - til - lion
La___ la la la___ la

back in the cit - y I been
squared___ the fight___ and she was
la___ la la la la

tak - en for lost___ and gone___
right___ in the rain___ of the
la___ la la la___ la la

D7

___ and un - known___ for a long,___ long time.
bul - lets that e - ven - tu - al - ly brought her down.___
la___ la la la___ la la la la.___

G7

___ Fell in love years a - go with an
___ But she's still danc - ing in the
___ Stand or fall, I know there shall be

CODA

vil - lains. ____

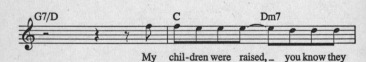

My chil-dren were raised, _ you know they

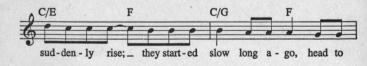

sud-den-ly rise; _ they start-ed slow long a - go, head to

toe, health-y, wealth-y and wise.
(Instrumental)

73

I GET AROUND

Words and Music by BRIAN WILSON
and MIKE LOVE

Medium bright Rock

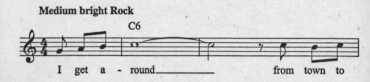

I get a - round_____ from town to

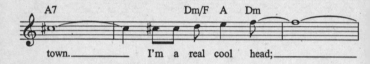

town._____ I'm a real cool head;_____

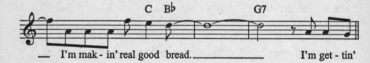

_ I'm mak - in' real good bread._____ I'm get - tin'

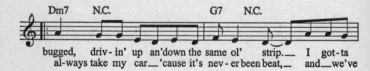

bugged, driv - in' up an' down the same ol' strip._ I got - ta
al - ways take my car_ 'cause it's nev - er been beat,_ and_ we've

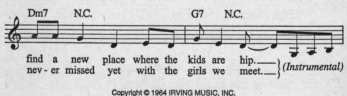

find a new place where the kids are hip._} *(Instrumental)*
nev - er missed yet with the girls we meet._}

{ My
{ None of the

Dm7 N.C.   G7   N.C.

bud-dies and me___ are get - tin' real well - known,___yeah,   the
guys__ go stead - y'cause it would-n't be right___ to leave your

Dm7 N.C.   G7   N.C.

bad guys know us and they leave us a - lone.___} I get a-
best girl   home on a   Sat - ur - day night.___}

C6   A7

round_____   from town to   town._____

            Dm/F   A   Dm

___ I'm   a   real   cool   head;_____

                    C   B♭

___ I'm   mak - in' real good bread._____

1   2   **Repeat and Fade**
G7   G7   C   Am

___   We _____

I JUST WASN'T MADE FOR THESE TIMES

Words and Music by BRIAN WILSON
and TONY ASHER

Moderately

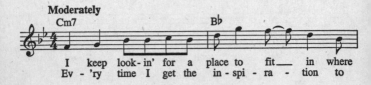

I keep look-in' for a place to fit___ in where
Ev-'ry time I get the in-spi-ra-tion to

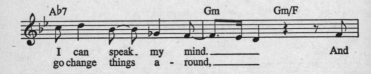

I can speak___ my mind._____
go change things a-round,_____ And

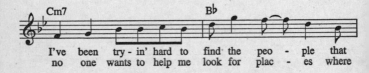

I've been try-in' hard to find the peo-ple that
no one wants to help me look for plac-es where

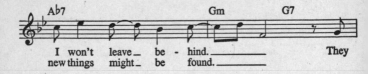

I won't leave___ be-hind._____
new things might___ be found._____ They

F

ver - y sad.
put my heart and soul in - to.

Cm7

Some - times I feel
Can't find noth - in' I can

F

ver - y sad.
put my heart and soul in - to.

Eb **A7** **G7sus** **G7b9**

(Instrumental)

Cm9 **F7/C** **Eb/F**

I guess I just was - n't made for these times.

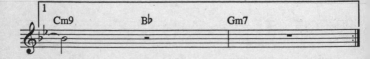

1

Cm9 **Bb** **Gm7**

79

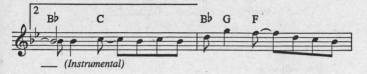

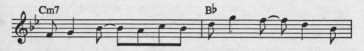

I guess I just was-n't made for these times.

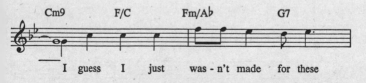

I guess I just was-n't made for these times.

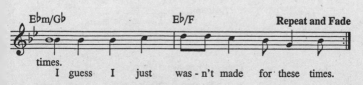

I guess I just was-n't made for these
times.
I guess I just was-n't made for these times.

IN MY ROOM

Words and Music by BRIAN WILSON
and GARY USHER

Moderately slow

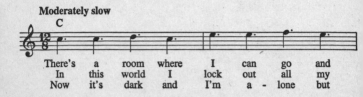

There's a room where I can go and
In this world I lock out all my
Now it's dark and I'm a - lone but

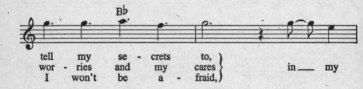

tell my se - crets to, }
wor - ries and my cares }
I won't be a - fraid, }   in ___ my

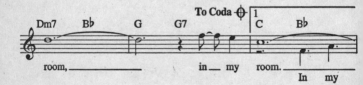

room, _____   in ___ my room.
                                         In my

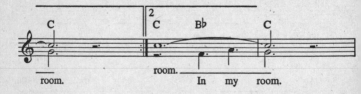

room.
          room.   In my room.

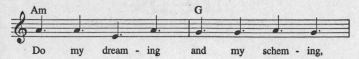

Do my dream - ing and my schem - ing,

lie a - wake and pray. ___ Do my cry - ing

D.C. al Coda

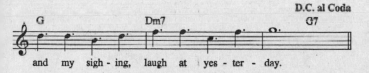

and my sigh - ing, laugh at yes - ter - day.

CODA

room In my room, in my room, in my

Room. ___

room, in my room, in my room.

IT'S OK

Words and Music by BRIAN WILSON
and MIKE LOVE

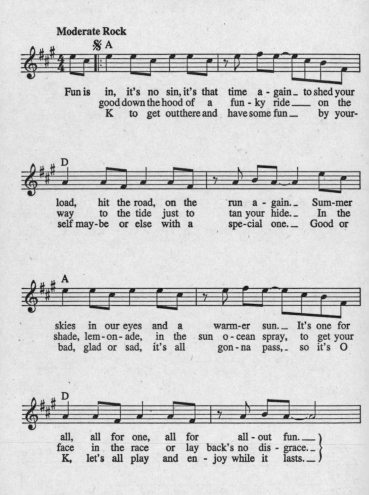

Moderate Rock

Fun is in, it's no sin, it's that time a - gain to shed your
good down the hood of a fun - ky ride on the
K to get out there and have some fun by your-

load, hit the road, on the run a - gain. Sum - mer
way to the tide just to tan your hide. In the
self may - be or else with a spe - cial one. Good or

skies in our eyes and a warm - er sun. It's one for
shade, lem - on - ade, in the sun o - cean spray, to get your
bad, glad or sad, it's all gon - na pass, so it's O

all, all for one, all for all - out fun.
face in the race or lay back's no dis - grace.
K, let's all play and en - joy while it lasts.

KEEP AN EYE ON SUMMER

Words and Music by BRIAN WILSON
and BOB NORBERG

Moderately

Keep an eye on sum - mer.

Keep an eye on sum - mer.
(Ah.)

We ___ said good-bye ___ last Sep - tem - ber.
Those ___ things I say ___ in my let - ters,

Your ___ words I still ___ can hear. ___ }
you'll ___ find they're all ___ sin - cere. ___ }

Keep an eye on sum - mer this year.
(Ah.)

year.

85

KOKOMO

Words and Music by MIKE LOVE, TERRY MELCHER,
JOHN PHILLIPS and SCOTT McKENZIE

Moderately bright

A - ru - ba, Ja - mai - ca, oo___ I wan - na take ya. Ber-

mu - da, Ba - ha - ma, come___ on, pret - ty ma - ma. Key

Lar - go, Mon - te - go, ba - by, why don't we we go, Ja-

mai - ca. Off the Flor - i - da Keys___
We'll put out to sea___

___ there's a place called Ko - ko - mo.___
And we'll per - fect our chem - is - try.___

88

mu - da,   Ba - ha - ma,   come on, pret - ty ma - ma.   Key

Lar - go,   Mon - te - go,   ba - by, why don't we go.

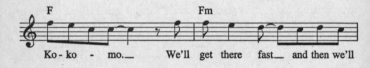

Ko - ko - mo.   We'll get there   fast and then we'll

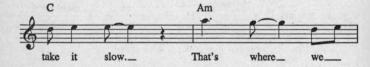

take   it   slow.   That's   where   we

wan - na go,   way down in Ko - ko - mo.

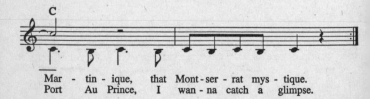

Mar - tin - ique,   that Mont - ser - rat mys - tique.
Port   Au Prince,   I   wan - na catch a   glimpse.

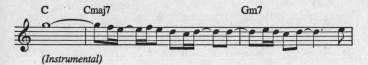

C   Cmaj7   Gm7

(Instrumental)

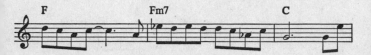

F   Fm7   C

D7   G7   C

Ev-'ry - bod-y knows

Cmaj7   Gm7   F

a lit - tle place like Ko - ko - mo.

Fm   C

Now if you wan - na go___ to get a -

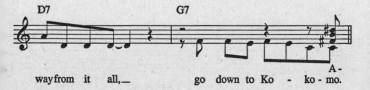

D7   G7

way from it all,___ go down to Ko - ko - mo.

A-

90

ru - ba, Ja - mai - ca, oo___ I wan-na take ya to Ber-

mu - da, Ba - ha - ma, come__ on, pret-ty ma-ma. Key

Oo_____ I wan - na take you down to

Lar - go, Mon - te - go, ba - by, why don't we go.

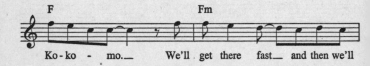

Ko - ko - mo.__ We'll get there fast__ and then we'll

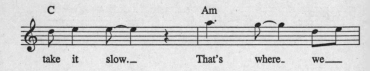

take it slow.__ That's where__ we__

Repeat and Fade

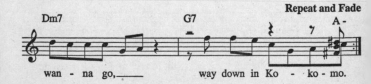

wan - na go,_____ way down in Ko - ko - mo.

LET HIM RUN WILD

Words and Music by BRIAN WILSON
and MIKE LOVE

Moderate Rock

When I watched you walk with him ___
do the same to oth - er girls ___ that
All the dreams you shared with him ___ you

tears filled my eyes, _____ and
he did to you, _____ but
might as well for - get. I

when I heard you talk with him ___
then one day he'll run in - to one
know you need a tru - er love ___

I could - n't stand his lies. _____
that's gon - na hurt him too. _____
and that's what you'll get. _____

And now be - fore he tries it, I hope you
Be - fore he makes you o - ver, I'm gon - na
And now that you don't need him, well, he can

92

LET'S GO AWAY
FOR A WHILE

Words and Music by
BRIAN WILSON

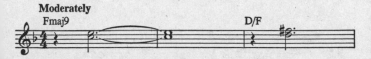

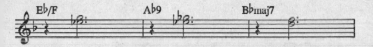

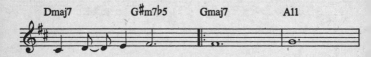

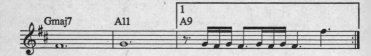

LITTLE DEUCE COUPE

Music by BRIAN WILSON
Words by ROGER CHRISTIAN

Moderate Rock

Well, I'm not brag-gin', babe, so don't put me down,— but I've got the fast-est set of wheels in town.— When some-thing pulls— up to me, it don't e-ven try,— and if it had a set of wings, man, I

lit-tle deuce coupe— with a flat-head mill,— but she'll walk a Thun-der-bird— like it's stand-in' still.— She's port-ed and re-lieved, and she's stroked and she's bored.— She'll do a hun-dred and— for-ty with the

97

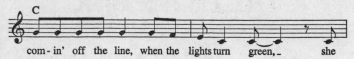

com-in' off the line, when the lights turn green, _ she

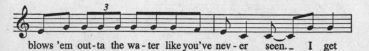

blows 'em out-ta the wa-ter like you've nev-er seen. _ I get

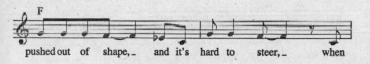

pushed out of shape, _ and it's hard to steer, _ when

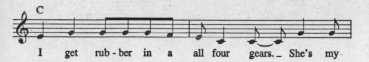

I get rub-ber in a all four gears. _ She's my

lit-tle deuce coupe, you don't know _ what I've got! _

She's got a

THE LITTLE GIRL
I ONCE KNEW

Words and Music by
BRIAN WILSON

Moderately

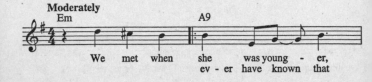

We met when she was young - er,
ev - er have known that

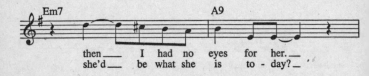

then___ I had no eyes for her.___
she'd___ be what she is to - day?___

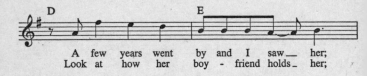

A few years went by and I saw___ her;
Look at how her boy - friend holds___ her;

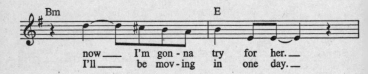

now___ I'm gon - na try for her.___
I'll___ be mov - ing in one day.___

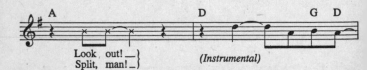

Look, out! ___ }
Split, man! ___ }   *(Instrumental)*

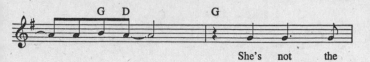

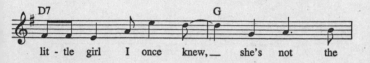

She's not the

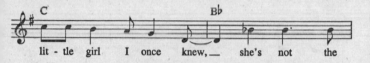

lit - tle girl I once knew, __ she's not the

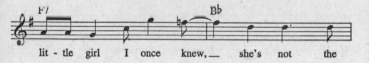

lit - tle girl I once knew, __ she's not the

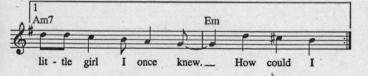

lit - tle girl I once knew, __ she's not the

lit - tle girl I once knew. __ How could I

lit - tle girl I once knew. __ *(Instrumental)*

100

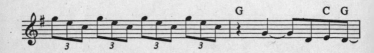

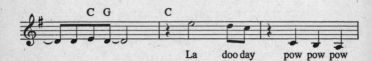

La   doo day   pow pow pow

pow. La   doo day   pow pow pow   pow. La   doo day

pow   pow   pow.   She's   not   the

lit - tle girl I once knew, ___ she's not   the

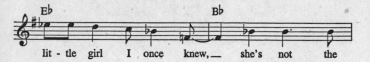

lit - tle girl I once knew, ___ she's not the

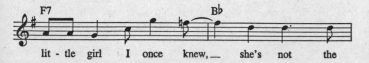

lit - tle girl I once knew, ___ she's not the

lit - tle girl I once knew. ___ *(Instrumental)*

She's not the

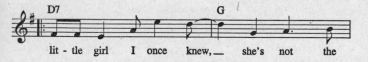

lit - tle girl I once knew, ___ she's not the

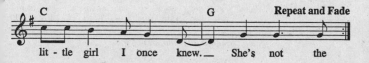

lit - tle girl I once knew. ___ She's not the

LITTLE HONDA

Words and Music by BRIAN WILSON
and MIKE LOVE

D

an - y - where you want me to. \
an - y - place I know you like. \
ride my Hon - da to - night. }

A % **D**

First gear, it's all right; —

G **D**

— sec - ond gear, — a - lean right; —

G **D**

— third gear, — hang on tight. —

G **A**

— Fast - er, — it's all

1, 2 | **3** **D.S. and Fade**

right. { It's not a   right.   First
{ It climbs the

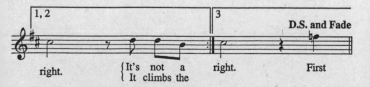

LITTLE SAINT NICK

Words and Music by BRIAN WILSON
and MIKE LOVE

Moderately fast

Well,_ way up north where the air gets cold,_ there's a
lit-tle bob-sled, we call it Old Saint Nick,_ but she'll
haul-in' through the snow at a fright-'nin' speed_ with a

tale a-bout Christ-mas that you've all been told._ And a
walk a to-bog-gan with a four speed stick._ She's
half a doz-en deer_ with_ Ru-dy to lead. He's

real fa-mous cat all dressed up in red,_ and he
can-dy ap-ple red with a ski for a wheel, and when
got-ta wear his gog-gles 'cause the snow real-ly flies, and he's

spends the whole_ year work-in' out on his sled._ }
San-ta hits the gas, man, just watch her_ peel._ } It's the
cruis-in' ev-'ry pad with a lit-tle sur-prise._ }

To Coda

Lit-tle Saint Nick. (Lit-tle Saint Nick.)_ It's the

1
D

Lit-tle Saint Nick. (Lit-tle Saint Nick.)_ Just a

Saint Nick.) Run, run, rein - deer. ___

___ Run, run, rein - deer.

Oh. ___ Run, run, rein - deer. ___

___ Run, run, rein deer. He

don't miss no one. And

Lit-tle Saint Nick. (Lit-tle

Saint Nick.) Ah, ___ Mer-ry Christ-mas, Saint ___

Nick. ___ (Christ - mas comes this time each year.) _ Ah, ___

THE MAN WITH ALL THE TOYS

Words and Music by BRIAN WILSON and MIKE LOVE

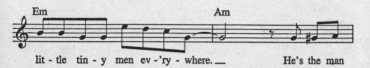

big man in a chair, ____ and

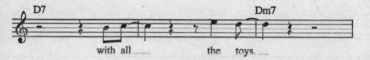

lit - tle tin - y men ev - 'ry - where. ____ He's the man

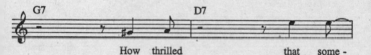

with all ____ the toys. ____

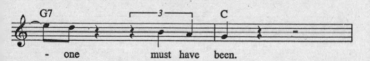

How thrilled that some -

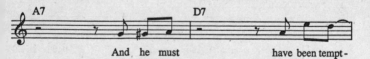

- one must have been.

And he must have been tempt -

- ed to go in. *(Instrumental)*

108

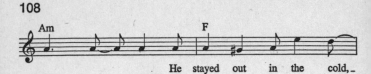

He stayed out in the cold,

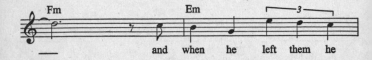

and when he left them he

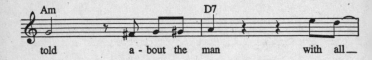

told a - bout the man with all

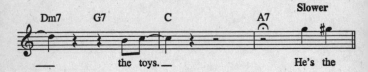

the toys. He's the

man with all the toys.

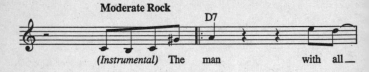

(Instrumental) The man with all

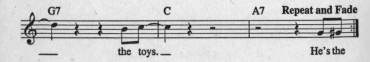

the toys. He's the

PET SOUNDS
By BRIAN WILSON

Moderately

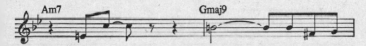

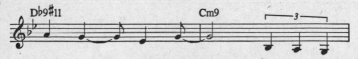

110
PLEASE LET ME WONDER

Words and Music by BRIAN WILSON
and MIKE LOVE

SALT LAKE CITY

Words and Music by BRIAN WILSON
and MIKE LOVE

Moderately

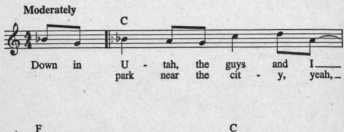

Down in U - tah, the guys and I____
park near the cit - y, yeah, ____

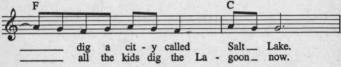

____ dig a cit - y called Salt__ Lake.
____ all the kids dig the La - goon__ now.

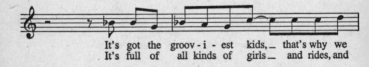

It's got the groov - i - est kids,__ that's why we
It's full of all kinds of girls__ and rides, and

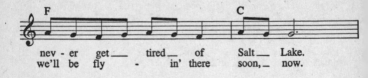

nev - er get__ tired__ of Salt__ Lake.
we'll be fly - in' there soon,__ now.

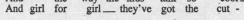

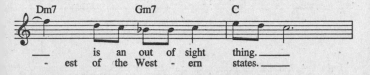

And   the   way the kids talk so   cool __
And girl for   girl __ they've got the   cut -

__   is   an out of sight   thing. __
- est of the West - ern   states. __

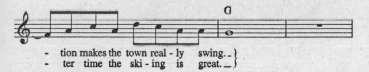

And the num-ber one   ra - di - o sta -
They got the   sun   in the sum-mer and win -

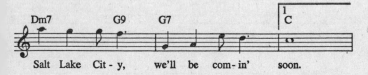

- tion makes the town real - ly   swing. __ }
- ter time the ski - ing is   great. __ }

Salt Lake Cit - y,   we'll be com-in'   soon.

There's a   soon. __

SHUT DOWN

Words by ROGER CHRISTIAN
Music by BRIAN WILSON

Bright Rock beat

Tach it up, tach it up, bud-dy, gon-na shut you down.

It

hap - pened on the strip where the
De - clin - in' num - bers at an
Ped - al's to the floor, hear his

road is wide, _____
e - ven rate, _____
dual quads drink, _____ and now the

two the cool shorts stand - in'
at the count of one we both ac -
Four Thir - teen's lead is

side by side.___ Yeah, my
cel - er - ate.___ My
start - in' to shrink.___ He's

C

fuel - in - ject - ed Sting - ray and a
Sting - ray is___ light, the slicks are
hot with ram - in - duc - tion, but it's

Four Thir - teen,___
start - in' to spin,___ but the
un - der - stood,___ I got a

G

rev - vin' up our en - gines and it
Four Thir - teen's___ real - ly
fuel - in - ject - ed en - gine sit - tin'

A

sounds real mean.___ Tach it up, tach it up,
dig - gin' in.___ Got - ta be cool now,
un - der my hood.___ Shut if off, shut it off,

Cm **D** **G** **To Coda** ⊕

bud - dy, gon - na shut you down.___
pow - er shift, here we go.___
bud - dy, now I shut you down.___

116

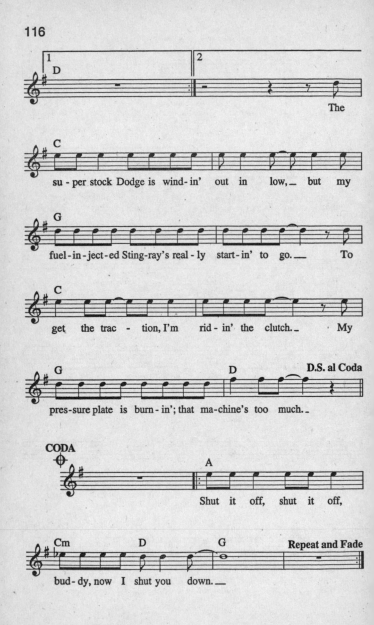

SLOOP JOHN B

Words and Music by
BRIAN WILSON

Moderately

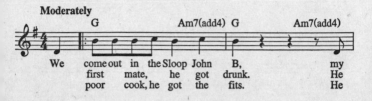

We come out in the Sloop John B, my
first mate, he got drunk. He
poor cook, he got the fits. He

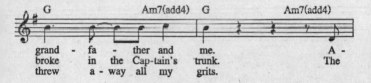

grand - fa - ther and me. A -
broke in the Cap-tain's trunk. The
threw a - way all my grits. The

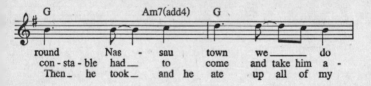

round Nas - sau town we do
con - sta - ble had to come and take him a -
Then he took and he ate up all of my

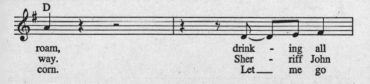

roam, drink - ing all
way. Sher - riff John
corn. Let me go

119

SPIRIT OF AMERICA

Words and Music by BRIAN WILSON
and ROGER CHRISTIAN

SURF'S UP

Words and Music by BRIAN WILSON
and VAN DYKE PARKS

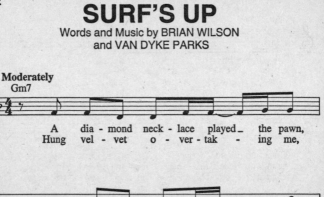

A dia-mond neck-lace played the pawn,
Hung vel-vet o-ver-tak-ing me,

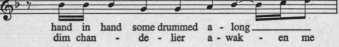

hand in hand some drummed a-long
dim chan-de-lier a-wak-en me

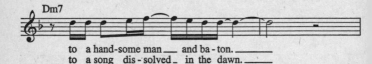

to a hand-some man and ba-ton.
to a song dis-solved in the dawn.

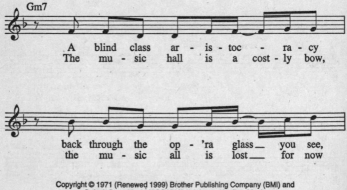

A blind class ar-is-toc-ra-cy
The mu-sic hall is a cost-ly bow,

back through the op-'ra glass you see,
the mu-sic all is lost for now

the pit ___ and the pen - du-lum drawn. _____ }
to a mut - ed trum - pet - er swan. _____ }

Col - on - nad - ed ru - ins dom - i -

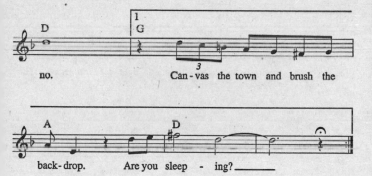

no.   Can - vas the town and brush the

back- drop.   Are you sleep - ing? _____

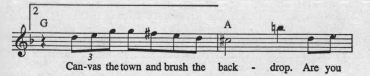

Can-vas the town and brush the   back - drop. Are you

sleep - ing, _____   Broth - er   John? _____

124

Dove-nest-ed towers the hour was,
Surf's up, mm, mm, mm, mm, mm,

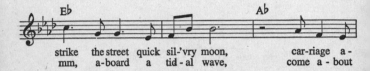

strike the street quick sil-'vry moon,   car-riage a-
mm, a-board a tid-al wave,   come a-bout

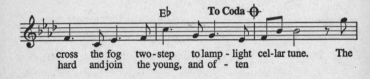

cross the fog two-step to lamp-light cel-lar tune. The
hard and join the young, and of-ten

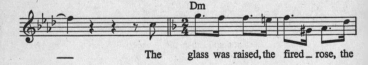

laughs come hard in auld lang syne.___

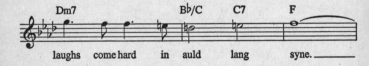

___ The glass was raised, the fired___ rose, the

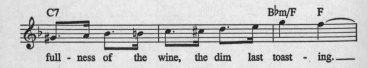

full-ness of the wine, the dim last toast-ing.___

While at port a - dieu or

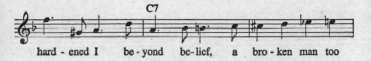

die._____ A choke of grief heart

hard - ened I be - yond be - lief, a bro - ken man too

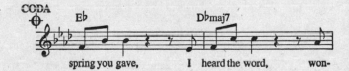

tough to cry _____

CODA

spring you gave, I heard the word, won-

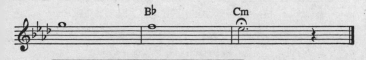

der - ful thing, a chil-dren's song. _____

Bb   Cm

SURFER GIRL

Words and Music by
BRIAN WILSON

SURFERS RULE

Words and Music by BRIAN WILSON
and MIKE LOVE

SURFIN' SAFARI

Words and Music by BRIAN WILSON
and MIKE LOVE

132

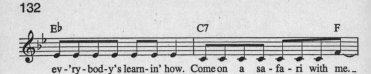

ev - 'ry - bod - y's learn - in' how. Come on a sa - fa - ri with me. __

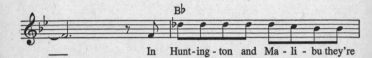

__ In Hunt - ing - ton and Ma - li - bu they're

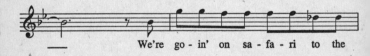

shoot - in' the pier, __ In Rin - con, they're walk - in' the nose. __

__ We're go - in' on sa - fa - ri to the

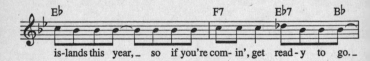

is - lands this year, __ so if you're com - in', get read - y to go. __

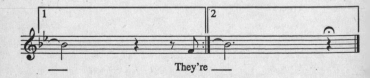

__ They're __

SURFIN' U.S.A.

Words and Music by
CHUCK BERRY

Solid Shuffle beat

If ev - 'ry - bod - y had an o - cean_____
route_____

— a - cross the U. S. A._____
we're gon - na take real soon._____

— Then ev - 'ry - bod - y'd be surf - in'_____
— We're wax - in' down__ our surf - boards._____

— like Cal - i - for - ni - a._____
— We can't wait for June._____

— You'd see them wear - in' their bag - gies,_____
— We'll all be gone for the sum - mer,_____

huar - a - chi san - dals too.
we're on sa - fa - ri to stay.

A bush - y bush - y blonde hair - do,
Tell the teach - er we're surf - in',

surf - in' U. S. A.
surf - in' U. S. A.

You'll catch 'em surf - in' at Del Mar
At Hag - gar - ty's and Swam - i's

Ven - tu - ra Coun - ty Line
Pa - cif - ic Pal - i - sades

San - ta Cruz and Tress - els,
San O - no - fre and Sun - set

135

Aus - tra - lia's Nar - a - bine _____
Re - don - do Beach, L. A. _____

All o - ver Man - hat - tan _____
All o - ver La Jol - la, _____

and down Do - he - ny way. _____
at Wai - a - me - a Bay. _____

Ev - 'ry - bod - y's gone surf - in' _____
Ev - 'ry - bod - y's gone surf - in' _____

surf - in' U. S. A. _____
surf - in' U. S. A. _____

We'll all be plan - nin' out a _____

THAT'S NOT ME

Words and Music by BRIAN WILSON
and TONY ASHER

I had to prove that I could
folks, when I wrote and I told them

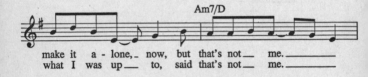

make it a - lone, now, but that's not me.
what I was up to, said that's not me.

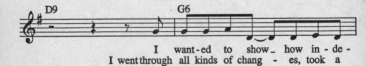

I want-ed to show how in - de -
I went through all kinds of chang - es, took a

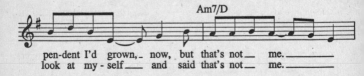

pen-dent I'd grown, now, but that's not me.
look at my - self and said that's not me.

____ much more sure that we're read - y. _____

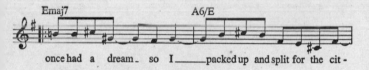

Do. _____ I

once had a dream_ so I_____packed up and split for the cit -

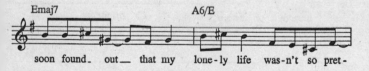

- y. _(Instrumental)_ I

soon found_ out__ that my lone - ly life was-n't so pret -

- ty. _(Instrumental)_ I

THE WARMTH OF THE SUN

Words and Music by BRIAN WILSON
and MIKE LOVE

What good is the dawn____ that grows in - to
love of my life, ____ she left me one

day? ____ The sun - set at night
day; ____ I cried when she said,

____ or liv - ing this way? ____ For I have the
____ "I don't feel the same way." ____ Still I'll have the

warmth_ of the sun, with - in me at
warmth_ of the sun, with - in me to -

1.
night. ____ The

2.
night. ____

WENDY

Words and Music by BRIAN WILSON
and MIKE LOVE

Moderately fast

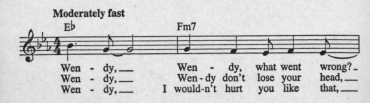

Wen - dy, ___ Wen - dy, what went wrong? ___
Wen - dy, ___ Wen - dy don't lose your head, ___
Wen - dy, ___ I would-n't hurt you like that, ___

___ Oh so wrong.
___ lose your head.
___ no, no, no.

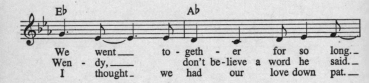

We went ___ to - geth - er for so long. ___
Wen - dy, ___ don't be - lieve a word he said. ___
I thought ___ we had our love down pat. ___

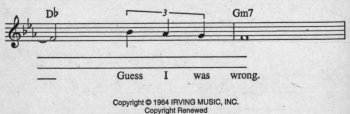

___ Guess I was wrong.

WHEN I GROW UP
(To Be a Man)
Words and Music by BRIAN WILSON and MIKE LOVE

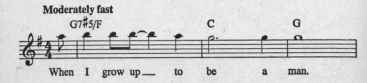

When I grow up__ to be a man.

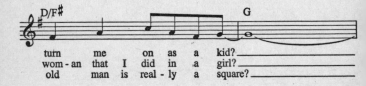

Will I dig the same__ things that
look for the same__ things in a
kids be proud__ or think their

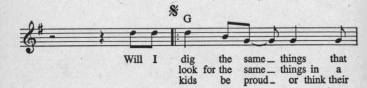

turn me on as a kid?_____
wom-an that I did in a girl?_____
old man is real-ly a square?_____

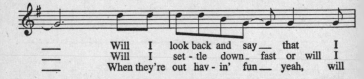

Will I look back and say__ that I
Will I set-tle down__ fast or will I
When they're out hav-in' fun__ yeah, will

146

man? _____ Ooh, _____

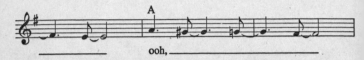

_____ ooh, _____

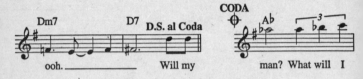

Dm7   D7   **D.S. al Coda**   **CODA**   Ab

ooh. _____ Will my   man? What will I

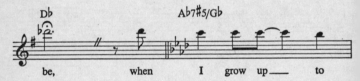

Db   Ab7#5/Gb

be,   when   I   grow up____   to

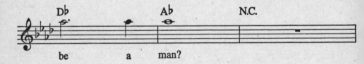

Db   Ab   N.C.

be   a   man?

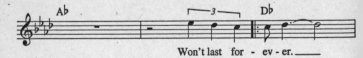

Ab   Db

Won't last for - ev - er.____

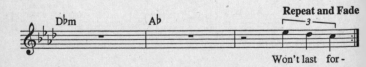

Dbm   Ab   **Repeat and Fade**

Won't last   for -

WILD HONEY

Words and Music by BRIAN WILSON
and MIKE LOVE

Bright Rock

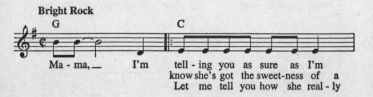

Ma - ma, __ I'm tell - ing you as sure as I'm
know she's got the sweet-ness of a
Let me tell you how she real - ly

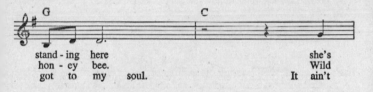

stand - ing here she's
hon - ey bee. Wild
got to my soul. It ain't

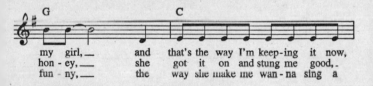

my girl, __ and that's the way I'm keep-ing it now,
hon - ey, __ she got it on and stung me good, _
fun - ny, __ the way she make me wan - na sing a

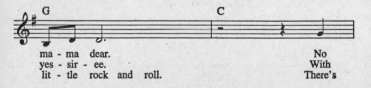

ma - ma dear. No
yes - sir - ee. With
lit - tle rock and roll. There's

Am   C

good will it do ___ you to stand there and frown ___ at me. The
all the oth - er stud bees buzz - ing all a - round her hive, she
noth-ing quite sweet ___ as a kiss of wild hon - ey. I

Am   C

girl's got my heart and my love's com in' down ___ on me. My
sin - gled me out, sin - gle - hand - ed took me ___ a - live. ___
break my back work - in' just to save me some mon - ey so

Am   D7

love's com - in' down since I got a taste of wild
Can you dig it? Gon - na take my life eat - in' up ___ wild
I can spend my life with ___ her. Sock it to me, wild

1.   2.
G   G   C

hon - ey. You hon - ey, wild

G   3.
                      G

hon - ey. ___ hon - ey. ___

WIND CHIMES

Words and Music by BRIAN WILSON
and VAN DYKE PARKS

WOULDN'T IT BE NICE

**Words and Music by BRIAN WILSON,
TONY ASHER and MIKE LOVE**

Moderate Shuffle

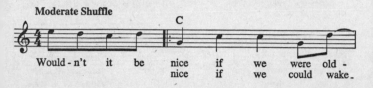

Would - n't it be nice if we were old -
nice if we could wake

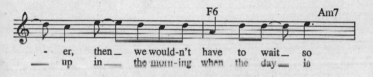

- er, then __ we would-n't have to wait __ so
__ up in __ the morn-ing when the day __ is

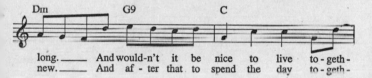

long. __ And would-n't it be nice to live to-geth-
new. __ And af-ter that to spend the day to-geth-

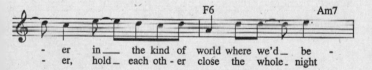

- er in __ the kind of world where we'd __ be -
- er, hold __ each oth - er close the whole __ night

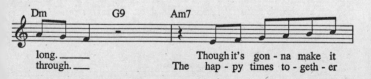

long. _____ Though it's gon - na make it
through. __ The hap - py times to - geth - er

G9   G11   C

oh would-n't it __ be __ nice. ____

Slower
C

Am7

You know, it seems the more we

C11   Am7

talk a - bout __ it. __ it on - ly makes it worse to

Em   Dm7   ⌐ 3 ┐   Em

live with-out __ it. ____ But let's talk a - bout __

Tempo I
Dm7   G9   G11

__ it. ____ Oh would-n't it __ be __

C   C   Repeat and Fade

__ nice. ____

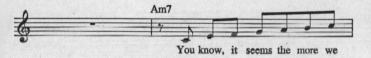
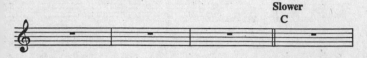

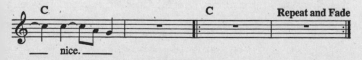

YOU'RE SO GOOD TO ME

Words and Music by BRIAN WILSON
and MIKE LOVE

Moderately

155

GUITAR CHORD FRAMES

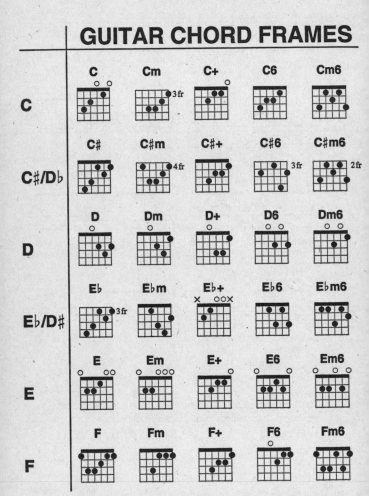

This guitar chord reference includes 120 commonly used chords. For a more complete guide to guitar chords, see "THE PAPERBACK CHORD BOOK" (HL00702009).

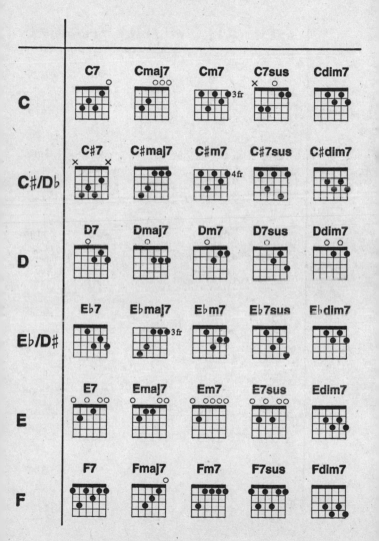

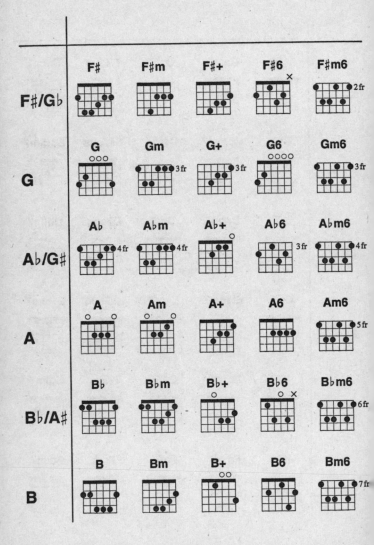

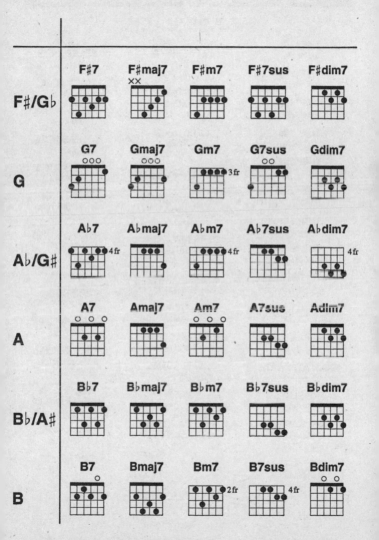

Prices, availability and contents subject to change without notice. Some products may not be available outside the U.S.A.